SAP IS-Retail Interview Questions, Answers, and Explanations

By: SAPCOOKBOOK.com

SAP IS-Retail Interview Questions Answers and Explanations

ISBN10: 1-933804-34-3
ISBN13:978-1-933804-34-7

Please visit our website at www.sapcookbook.com

Table of Contents

Introduction

SAP Retail is a completely integrated retailing system. It maps the complete set of business processes required for competitive assortment strategies, different retail formats, and ECR-driven logistics and distribution. It provides all the functions necessary for modeling business processes in a retail company.

With SAP Retail, SAP has endeavored to model the full "Value Chain", all the links in the logistics pipeline from consumer to vendor. Retailers can thus optimize the whole array of business processes and control checks in managing the flow of merchandise and information among vendors, retailers, and consumers.

The business process area "Retailing" comprises the procurement, storage, distribution, and sale of merchandise. SAP Retail supports both wholesale and retail scenarios.

The Retail Information System (RIS) enables goods movements to be planned, monitored, and tracked throughout the whole supply chain.

The key retailing processes include:

- Assortment Management
- Sales Price Calculation
- Promotion Management
- Allocation
- Requirements Planning and Purchasing
- Goods Receipt
- Invoice Verification and Subsequent Settlement of End-Of-Period Arrangements
- Warehouse Management
- Picking and Delivery
- Billing
- Store Supply

The retailing processes enable you to control and coordinate the whole value chain, and thus react swiftly to changes in consumer behavior.

New trends, such as electronic commerce or ECR, flow continually into ongoing development cycles. SAP Retail also allows for changes in legal structures or business practices – franchising, for example. This ensures that retailers not only have a future-proof investment but are able to adapt swiftly to a changing market. The growth of your company is not hampered by system constraints, and you can incorporate changes in the real world smoothly and efficiently into the system.

Question 1: IS-Retail Coupons

If we take a business scenario in which there are coupons published in newspaper and customer takes the cutting to store to buy articles.

At POS when he presents coupons, POS gets details of coupons from SAP in form of IDoc, based on this, customer can avail a discount of X% on Apparel and Footwear Merchandise Category (MC). This percentage offer is not applicable for other MCs.

Now where and how can we create these bonus buy promotions in SAP (i.e. How are these coupons created and how are they linked to promotions)?

A: These coupons are created in IS-Retail using MM41. Then you can use it in the bonus buy functionality as any other article. To limit the use of coupons to the Apparel and Footwear Merchandise Category you will have to create a material grouping including just these categories. The bonus buy condition will use the material grouping to grant the coupons.

Question 2: IS-Retail Buy One Get One Free

Is it possible to solve the following scenario through SAP- Retail:

If you buy two books, you will get the cheaper one free?

A: The bonus buy functionality in IS-Retail can be used to solve this case. You can create a bonus buy via a retail promotion or via sales condition master data.

If you first create a material grouping with all the articles in the combination, and then you create the bonus buy condition using that material grouping.

Check the bonus buy customizing in IMG ---> Sales and distribution ---> Basic functions ---> Bonus.

Question 3: Transaction MM43 in Industrial System

What is equivalent Transaction of MM43 of the Retail-System in the Industrial System?

A: The equivalent Transaction of MM43 of the Retail-System in the Industrial System is MM03.

Question 4: IS-R HPR

What is the use of HPR (High Performance Retail)?

A: HPR in Retail consists of programs specifically on the SAP to POS/BOS interface to improve the runtime of Master data (e.g. Article master/assortment list) IDoc generation. These programs are more efficient than the standard SAP programs. However, the end results are not exactly identical and certain enhancements are also not available in HPR.

Question 5: Cost of Bulk Breaking

If you are purchasing a Sugar Bag of 100 kg and in warehouse, you are packing it in pieces of 1 Kg each. How can you account for the cost that has incurred in W/H (i.e. How can you account for the cost of Bulk Breaking in SAP-IS-Retail)?

A: It can be done through a couple of workarounds. First, using a little bit of PP. You can setup a production order, which consumes the Sugar in bulk bags and produces Sugar in 1 Kg bags. You can do costing on this and settle it to the finished product to get accurate costs. This will handle both the stock movement and also cost calculation.

Alternatively, you can have an additional surcharge condition type (e.g. packaging costs) that applies a fixed amount or % of cost to the specific products whenever the sell price (VKP0) is calculated. This is simpler and a one-off exercise that requires almost no maintenance on a day-to-day basis.

Question 6: WM Replenishment

How SAP runs replenishment for the locations in a warehouse, which are used for sales and when the stock is lower in these locations, the stock from other locations are moved there?

A: SAP WM perfectly manages this scenario. This will take several steps:

1. Define a fixed bin putway strategy for the warehouse/storage type (customizing for WM).
   Also consider the need for a "reserve" storage type from where the "picking" (i.e. "sales" in this case) storage type will replenish.
2. Define Replenishment control for the warehouse or storage type (customizing for WM).
   Here you will define the movement type (you can use 319) for the replenishment and the replenishment method (via report or immediately).
3. Maintain the material master data (wm view) with the fixed storage, the maximum and minimum quantities (this is the data that will be used by the replenishment process) and the storage strategies (here you will control that from which storage type the material is going to replenish).
4. Now schedule the run of LP21. This will create all the transfer reqs to replenish the bins.

Question 7: Vendor Hierarchy without IS-Retail

Is it possible to implement vendor hierarchy without IS-Retail?

A: Yes, it is possible to Implement vendor hierarchy without SAP IS-Retail.

You can implement it by creating hierarchy nodes using acct GRP 0012. If you are implementing with a pre-configured client then there is little in the way configuration needed (i.e. You need to configure the following):

- Categories
- Partner determination
- Assign acct GRPS
- Assign PORG
- Assign hierarchy per Doc type

Question 8: Agency Business

Is it necessary to have the Retail solution in order to implement "Agency Business"?

A: Yes, IS-Retail should be activated for implementation of Agency Business.

Question 9: Loans Management

Can the Loans Management component of SAP (CML) be used by retail organizations that have pretty extensive loan activities or it is suitable just for banks?

A: TR-LM is a functionality that is capable to handle internal loans, external loans given or obtained. It is also capable to link internal and external loans (company-sponsored loans to employees). It is not just for bank and if you have SAP All-In-One license you should be able to implement and utilize it without additional fees (except consulting to implement). SAP Knowledge Warehouse gives the detailed idea about Loan Management component of SAP (CML).

Question 10: IS-Retail

What are the front-end POS solutions available in India for IS-Retail.

A: SAP does not require a specific POS for IS-Retail for India or any other country. It just needs to integrate with POS through IDoc/online.

Question 11: Rough GR

What is the function of rough GR?

A: The rough goods receipt (rough GR) is a step that takes place before the actual goods receipt posting. The delivery is identified and the items on the delivery documents sent by the vendor are matched up with the order items in the system. The system compares the quantities ordered with those contained in the delivery papers. This enables us to identify large quantity differences or articles that are wrongly delivered even before we take physical receipt of the goods.

Technically, a rough goods receipt document is the same as an inbound delivery. Only after the goods are physically received and the goods receipt posted, are the articles included in the inventory of the site. When the goods receipt is entered, reference is made to the rough goods receipt.

One can only use rough goods receipts through SAP Retail.

Question 12: Unit of Measurement

How can you assign alternate unit of measurement for a material for which Purchase Orders are created and Goods Receipt and Invoice Receipt have been done. ?

A: To assign alternate unit of measurement you need to go to the material master. On all screens in the material master you will find the 'Unit of measure' button. Press it and you can enter as many units (with a conversion factor to the Base Unit of measurement) as you want. This can be done independent of PO, stock, etc.

Question 13: Defining Material Groups

How can you create material groups that are not linked to a material master and can still have a material group hierarchy?

A: The core SAP system does not have the hierarchy function for the material group field. Therefore, you should build the hierarchy into the material group number itself because SAP Retail System allows a material group hierarchy.

In Release 4.0, 4.5 and 4.6, you can set your R/3 system as an SAP Retail System under the following conditions:

1. You are in possession of a valid SAP Retail license.
2. You want to use the processes, terminology, and documentation of the SAP Retail applications.
3. You accept that you cannot use certain manufacturing-oriented processes in an SAP Retail system.
4. You are fully aware that you cannot deactivate SAP Retail subsequently in the current Release.

Question 14: SAP HR in Retail

What are the typical requirements from the SAP HR system apart from PA and Payroll in a retail environment?

A: Following are the Key requirements from the SAP HR system:

- Human Resources
- Organizational Management:
  Organizational plan
  Expert mode
- Personnel Management:
  Administration
  Recruitment
  Personnel Development
- Time Management:
  Shift Planning
  Administration
  Time Sheet
- Payroll:
  Simulation
  Pay run
  Posting to Accounting

Question 15: Stock Initialization - using 2lis_40_s278

If you try to initialize stock using 2lis_40_s278 and get the following message:

"Inactive enhancement for BW extraction! Extraction not possible!

Message no. MCBW 014 "

What does it mean, and how can you fix the problem?

A: To fix the problem you should go to the BW IMG in R/3 (SBIW) and navigate the following path:

Settings for Application-Specific data sources ->
Logistics ->
Settings for IBU Retail ->
Determine Industry Sector

There you can change the SAP BW Usage indicator from "None" to "Retail".

This will fix the problem.

Question 16: Bonus Buy

How can you configure and activate "Bonus Buy" in SAP?

A: There is a retail functionality called bonus buy. Where you can set up all different kinds of conditions (i.e. If a coupon is used in at least three of the one material and two of the other, anything bought will be cheaper by 30%). It IS-Retail functionality and designed to download those conditions to the POS Systems of the retail stores. It is not meant to be used during price determination in SAP. Therefore, it cannot be used in a sales order.

Question 17: Additional EAN Scanning in Picking or Packing

If the "primary" EAN numbers are scanned properly but the additional EANs do not seem to work, does it indicate some configuration error?

A: It could be a configuration issue as EANs work well with IS-Retail as well as base SAP systems, weather it is primary or additional EANs. If such problem arises you should check your EAN data in table MEAN (using transaction SE16) and verify that the data has been correctly maintained

Question 18: Physical Inventory

What are the maximum number of lines those can be entered in a physical inventory document so that when this physical inventory document is posted (MI07) system will not give any errors?

A: The maximum number of lines those can be entered in a physical inventory document are 333. If entered more the system might create up to 3 items per physical inventory document item in the accounting document, when you post inventory differences. Therefore since the number of the items in a FI document is limited to 999, the number of the items in the physical inventory document must not be larger than 333.

Question 19: PBS-tool and Industry Solution Retail

Is there a PBS-tool that manages the Industry Solution Retail?

A: No, there is no PBS add-on for IS-Retail. Most of their add-ons are for the core modules that the majority of SAP customers use.

Question 20: Auto Create

Is it possible for a Retail company to have delivery and billing created automatically when the cashier generates a sales order?

If so, how is it done in SAP?

A: In standard 4.6 (probably earlier versions also), there is a standard SD document type for Cash Sales. Doc type BV - creates the delivery on the spot and a receipt. The Actual FI postings in billing happen during batch processing.

Question 21: HR in Retail Industry

How can you implement SAP HR in the retail industry? Does it need special knowledge of industry specific HR functions or is it a kind of a vanilla implementation like all other implementations?

A: No, it has no specific things on SAP HR that would only be used by the Retail Sector. In spite, there are different appraisal models, pay models, etc. However, those too will not be commonly used throughout the retail environment.

Question 22: Material Percentage

How can you calculate the percentage of one material in a given package that consists of 4-5 materials and is used for trade promotion purposes? Which SAP facility can be used?

A: It can be done through sales split and from 4.6a onwards. Bonus buy function will work.

Following are the Scope of Functions:

You can define conditions that only apply when the prerequisites and requirements you define are met. For example, you offer a reduced price when a customer buys certain quantities of particular materials together or when a credit card is used for payment. Here prerequisites can be items that have to be in a transaction in addition to the subject of the condition (i.e.; a prerequisite might be the purchase of other materials or the redemption of a coupon). Whereas requirements refer to the total sale in general or to other aspects of the sale (such as a minimum sale or payment by customer card).

You can enter a particular number of a single material or you can group together materials of your choice in any quantity as prerequisites. The subject of the condition can also be a single material, a group of materials, all the prerequisites, or even the whole transaction. Conditions can be special prices, fixed discounts, percentage discounts or free-goods discounts.

You can also define scales for the bonus buy condition. A distinction is made in R/3 between the following types of Bonus Buy:

<u>Multi-deal</u>:
At least one of the prerequisites must be met for the bonus buy to apply.

The following two examples illustrate how multi-deals are typically used:

1. CDs on a particular rack cost $ 5 each, but you offer any 3 CDs for only $ 10.
2. When customers buy any 3 CDs on special or one particular CD, you offer them 10% discount on a CD player of their choice.

<u>Combination deals</u>:
All the prerequisites defined for the Bonus Buy have to be met.

The following example illustrates how a combination deal is typically used:

When a customer buys a pair of skis and a pair of boots, you offer them a free pair of sunglasses.

You can transfer the prerequisites, requirements, and conditions for Bonus Buys to the POS systems (see Release Information POS Interface-Outbound: Integration of Bonus Buys).

At POS inbound processing, R/3 posts the Bonus Buys at the special conditions (see Release Information POS Interface-Inbound: Integration of Bonus Buys).

Question 23: Can a Sales Order BOM be triggered through POS Sales Interface

Is it possible to configure the inbound sales interface to trigger a sales order BOM if the article (material) has been set up as a header BOM item?

Given that you are using IDoc type WPUBON01 and have configured SAP sales order process so that pricing and billing are on the header article, but inventory/delivery are on the component articles. Because of which the desired outcome is billing document created for the item sold and article (material) document for the components.

A: By using a POS sales interface you cannot trigger the sales order BOM functionality, since you are getting into SAP at the moment of billing and inventory posting.

The sales order BOM can only be exploded during sales order entry. At billing, all the materials with a sales BOM should have been "exploded".

Question 24: Stock Transfer

How to handle stock transfer (company provided stock) from one sales representative to another in SAP? In the following scenario:

If as a part of retail business you have multiple sales representatives and you have created sales representatives as customers in SAP and have consignment orders. Before selling, the stocks are as consignment stocks and they are under sales representatives name.

Is it possible to transfer the stock from one sales representative to another? In other words is it possible to transfer the stock from one consignment to another?

A: No, a direct transfer from one consignment stock to another is not possible within the SAP Standard system.

In SAP, consignment stocks are assigned to specific customers. The normal process would be to perform a consignment Pick-Up Delivery from Customer A and a consignment Fill-Up Delivery to Customer B.

Question 25: Material Master

If you have SAP Retail solutions for a material/store, in which by mistake one of the users activates the purchasing view with reference to G.

Is there any way you can deactivate the purchasing view WRT to the vendor for the material/store or what should be done if it keeps on showing up in M_KREDM view even after deletion?

A: It is possible that only the deletion flag for info record is set. This does not mean that the info record is gone. It is just flagged for deletion (say archiving). You need to run SARA and archive object MM_EINA to get rid of the info record.

Question 26: SAP IDES

What is SAP IDES?

A: IDES – the "Internet Demonstration and Evaluation System" in the R/3 System, represents a model company. It consists of an international group with subsidiaries in several countries. IDES contains application data for various business scenarios that can be run in the SAP System. The business processes in the IDES system are designed to reflect real-life business requirements, and have access to many realistic characteristics. IDES uses easy-to-follow business scenarios to show you the comprehensive functions of the R/3 System. The focal point of IDES, however, is not the functionality itself, but the business processes and their integration.

Question 27: LSMW Query

If an LSMW is created to upload a file which will serve to create materials or to change existing materials using MM41 (create material-retail) and MM42 (change material-retail) now if a project, sub-project and two objects are created using recordings for MM41 and MM42 respectively. However, the condition is that standard SAP objects cannot be used for material creation as they are for MM01.

Now is there some way of processing the file to screen out the records which involve material change separately into an internal table (and probably flush them to the application server), and then at the end of the create material processing, one can somehow call the other recording object for material change? Alternatively, is their any other better way to go about it?

A: Yes, within your conversion code it is possible to perform a lookup against MARA to determine whether the material exists. You can output (using conventional ABAP) all the new record details to a log file as they are processed, together with the SKIP TRANSACTION command to jump over that particular record. You can then process the log file using a different LSMW script that creates them.

Question 28: IS-Retail –starter

Is there a general guide for SAP Retail, which is not just for beginners?

A: The SAP Best Practice for IS-Retail can be helpful for advance stage SAP users.

Question 29: Keeping up to Speed

Briefly describe the following:

1. BADI
2. IS- Retail (Utilities, etc)
3. EBP
4. APO
5. SEM

A:

1. BADI stands for Business Add In. It uses ABAP Objects and enables the same entry point to be used several times i.e. replaces the user exit.
2. IS stands for Industry Solution i.e. SAP specific solution for that industry.
3. EBP stands for Enterprise Buyer Professional an Internet-based procurement system that has been tailored specifically for the purchase of consumable materials in the public sector.
4. APO stands for Advanced Planner and Optimizer. It is designed to help a company in improving production planning, pricing, scheduling, and product shipping.
5. SEM stands for Strategic Enterprise Management supports and enables strategic management processes such as strategic planning, resource allocation, risk management, performance management, and value communication.

Question 30: IS-Retail 4.7

A company has upgrade the SAP IS-Retail from 4.0 to 4.7? Is there any major difference in the functionality?

A: There are BIG differences in functionality between 4.7 (R/3 Enterprise) and any previous release. Most of the enhancements are focused on High Performance Retailing in these areas:

- Archiving
- Article master
- Allocation
- Assortment
- Assortment list
- Collective Purchase Order
- Data migration
- Delivery
- [European Monetary Union]
- Forecast
- Investment buy
- Invoice verification
- Job scheduling
- LIS / RIS
- Listing
- Load build
- Merchandise Category
- Number Ranges
- POS Download
- POS Upload
- Price determination
- Pricing
- Promotion
- Physical Inventory Documents
- Purchase Order
- Replenishment (DC)
- Replenishment (Store)
- Retail MARC
- Shipping
- Subsequent Settlement
- Supply source determination
- Valuation at Retail

Question 31: SAP IDoc to ASCII File

How can you convert SAP IDoc to flat ASCII files to be read by other systems without using ABAP for the conversion? How can it be done with SAP Retail?

A: There can be two ways to convert SAP IDoc to flat ASCII files:

1. You can use Business connector, which has built in services to convert IDoc type to any preferred format, including ASCII flat file.
2. Or you can define an RFC path that writes the IDoc to the specified directory.

Question 32: SD Business Content

If all the information needed is present in oSD_Co1 and in oSD_Co3 also, and if one prefers to activate oSD_Co3 does he still need to go for oSD_Co1? What is the difference between these two cubes? Moreover if oSD_Co3 has data from Sales Orders, Billing and Delivery, what is the good/general practice?

To create separate cubes for Sales Orders, Billing and Shipping, then create a multi-provider on these cubes OR to go with oSD_Co3 (i.e. a single cube)?

A: With separate cubes you have the opportunity to enhance/reload each cube independently, and enhance the multi-provider to change the view. Whereas SD_Co1 is not only loaded from multiple sources, which makes the above mentioned process more difficult, it is also a very basic view of sales compared with the extractors it uses.

SD business content cubes are too basic and the sales view of organizations is too complex to make it easier for designing a custom cube than extending BC. SD extractors work great after little extension to meet the needs of all wide range of customers.

Question 33: Delivery Note Creation Log

If you have to send alerts to the sales order creator about the failure of delivery note creation, whenever it occurs, and there is a problem that if you try the V_SA it just can't filter by the sales order creator because a specific ID creates the DN in background. Is there any other report which can be used to list the delivery creation log?

A: Yes, you can try TCODE WF80 for listing the delivery creation log.

Question 34: User Exit for MM42/43

Is there a user exit that can be used before saving the data to validate the Alternative Unit of Measure of a material at POS tab/screen, or is there a way to make the Alternative Unit of Measure as "BLANK", because just filling this field makes all other fields as required fields?

A: Check this:

Automatic tool finds for MM42/43
Exit Name Description
MGW00001 Material Master (Retail): Additional Data
MGW00002 Material Master (Retail): Number Assignment

Question 35: Recommendation Courses for an Upgrade

What courses are needed to update the user to work on the following platform?

R/3 40B Retail
Oracle 9.2.0.5
W2003 server
Especially in DB, R/3 administration and configuration

A: You can take the following courses:

- SAP20 - General Vision
- SAP50 - Basis Tech
- BC305 - Advanced R/3 Admin
- BC325 - Work Organizer
- BC340 - Going Live
- BC505 - DB Admin
- SAP81 - 40B OSS

At least every year the 5+2+1 support ends and you need to migrate and update skills.

Question 36: Movement Types

What are the link/documents for consolidated documentation of Movement types?

A: Link/documents for consolidated documentation of Movement types:

1. 101 Goods receipt for purchase order or order.
2. If the purchase order or order has not been assigned to an account, a stock type (unrestricted-use stock, stock in quality inspection, blocked stock) can be entered during goods receipt.
3. If the purchase order or order has been assigned to an account, the goods receipt is not posted to the

warehouse, but to consumption. In the case of non-valuated materials, the goods receipt is posted to the warehouse, although the purchase order has not been assigned to an account.

4. Possible special stock indicators:
   a. K Goods receipt for purchase order to consignment stock
   b. O Goods receipt for purchase order to stock of material provided to vendor
   c. E GR for purchase order or order to
   d. Sales order stock
   e. Q GR for purchase order or order to
   f. Project stock.

5. Goods receipt for subcontract order: At goods receipt, the consumption of the components is posted at the same time (see movement type 543).

6. Goods receipt for stock transport order:
   a. At goods receipt the transported quantity is posted in the receiving plant from stock in transit into unrestricted-use stock (or stock in quality inspection, blocked stock).

7. 103 Goods receipt for purchase order into GR blocked stock you cannot receive goods into goods receipt blocked stock for stock transport orders.
   a. Possible special stock indicators: K, O, E, Q

8. 105 Release from GR blocked stock for purchase order. Movement type 105 has the same effects as 101.
   a. Possible special stock indicators: K, O, E, Q

9. 121 Subsequent adjustment for subcontracting. This movement type cannot be entered manually. With a subsequent adjustment for a subcontract order it is possible to correct the consumption of components. In this case, the material produced by the supplier is credited with the excess consumption / under-consumption. For this reason, if there is a subsequent adjustment, an item is generated for the produced material using movement type 121. Movement type 121 does not have a reversal movement type.
   a. Possible special stock indicators: O, E, Q

10. 122 Return delivery to supplier or to production. Using movement type 122, you can distinguish real return deliveries for a purchase order or order from cancellations (102). In the standard version, you must

enter a reason for the return delivery if you are using movement type 122. This enables you to carry out evaluations for return deliveries. The effects of movement type 122 correspond to a cancellation of movement type 101.

    a. Possible special stock indicators: K, O, E, Q

11. 123 Reversal of return delivery. If you returned a goods receipt using movement type 122, you can reverse the return delivery using movement type 123. This movement type has the same effects as movement type 101.

    a. Possible special stock indicators: K, O, E, Q

12. 124 Return delivery to vendor from GR blocked stock. Using movement type 124; you can return a goods receipt to GR blocked stock (103). Movement type 124 has the same effects as movement type 104.

    a. Possible special stock indicators: K, O, E, Q

13. 125 Return delivery from GR blocked stock–reversal. If you returned a goods receipt to GR blocked stock using movement type.

14. 124 You can reverse the return delivery using movement type 125. Movement type 125 has the same effects as movement type 103.

    a. Possible special stock indicators: K, O, E, Q

15. 131 Goods receipt for run schedule header. This movement type cannot be entered manually. It is generated automatically at notification of goods receipt for a run schedule header.

    a. Possible special stock indicators: E, Q

16. 141 Goods receipt for subsequent adjustment for active ingredient. This movement type cannot be entered manually. It is generated automatically upon subsequent adjustment for a proportion/product unit. Subsequent adjustment is necessary if the system finds that there has been excess consumption or under-consumption after a goods receipt posting.

    a. Possible special stock indicators: K, O, E, Q

17. 161 Return for purchase order. If a purchase order item is marked as a returns item, the returns to vendor are posted using movement type 161 when the goods receipt for purchase order (101) is posted. Movement type 161 has the same effects as movement type 122.

Question 37: Special Orders

How can you have other handled article numbers for Special Orders (i.e. same item but different sizes or different colors without creating multiple article numbers in the Article Master)?

A: This is handled by using 'Generic and Variants' article category and this is a standard IS-Retail feature.

You can check out the 'Articles: Generic Articles and Variants' at following link:

http://help.sap.com/saphelp_470/helpdata/en/50/94f500470e 11d1894a0000e8323352/frameset.htm

Question 38: What is PB00?

What is PB00?

A: PB00 is a condition type with the condition category H (Basic price) and it must always exist in the calculation schema. With Stock transfers as an exception.

Question 39: Deltas for APO from Info Cubes

Is there a way to upload delta records on APO without changing past data?

A: You can write a routine in the update rules using the following logic:

If date on record < System Date, delete package.

Then you will always get any deltas for any date more than system date, (i.e. any future date). That way, your past data will remain intact.

Question 40: Automatic Document Price Adjustment

If the following problem occurs while trying to use the Automatic Document Price Adjustment for PO:

When you run the transaction MEI4 (Create Work list), the system returns the following message: "No work list generated for document category 'Purchase order/scheduling agreement' (no changes)".

Then what is the right procedure for doing this?

A: Check for the following settings:

1. XK02 - doc index indicator flagged for vendor.
2. IMG- purch/conditions - check table entries 17 and 18 for PB00 and Origin for Condition 2 (pricing).
3. IMG- activate change pointer for CONDBI. Activate the CONDBI indicator.

If all set in the above stated manner then try with your own PO's. Make sure that they do not have any follow-on documents (such as GR, IR etc.) Check if Base condition type is PB00 in your PO, if not, set it to PB00.

Question 41: POS Outbound Trigger

Why it happens that while doing WPMI all Articles flow to POS whether they are listed or not, and when you do WPMA only listed articles flow to POS?

A: The setting for POS outbound profile for the parameter 'Sale permitted for all Art Groups' located on the right side under 'Additional Settings'. Should not be ticked if you want to output only listed articles.

Question 42: Regarding Help.sap.com on SAP BW

Where can you find the entire BW help from ADW to Enhancements?

A: You can try the following link for support:

Go to http://service.sap.com/

Question 43: One-time Vendor not Allowed in Material Master Record

What should be done if you create an account group for one-time vendor, and then you create material with MM41, after which in purchasing view you cannot set that one-time vendor to the material as it shows the following message "One-time vendor not defined" or "It does not make sense to allow a one-time vendor in this situation".

A: One-time vendor is for the following purposes:

1. One-time vendor as the name suggests is used only once as you may not buy from them again or you have not accepted them as your long term Vendor.
2. In the PO, it could be used for many different vendors, which you have not created into Vendor master record yet.

Therefore, if you are buying frequently from this vendor for this Stock Item Material, you should create a Vendor Record for it instead of using a One-time vendor.

Question 44: IS-Retail 'Requirement Planning' Run

What is the specific configuration settings required to run MRP at generic material level in IS-Retail?

A: Generic articles are holding articles in retails; therefore you cannot order/stock/sell these articles.

You can use these to maintain MRP parameters for the linked variants (Like MRP type etc). However, the actual consumption and MRP is executed for the variants only.

Question 45: MRP Types

What is the difference between MRP types PD & RP?

A: PD is a deterministic MRP, which means it will create requirements for demand, will do planned and unplanned consumption planning. Whereas, RP was developed for the Retail industry it is like a VB or a VM. Among them PD is the most popular one and it covers all bases.

Question 46: PSA-tables (How much space do they take)

How much space do PSA-tables have in an existing BW System and how can you see that in the System?

A: It depends on the type of Database. If it is Oracle, Trans DB02 lets you see the table spaces. The PSA data is in the table space ending ODS (it is a throw back to a previous version where PSA was called ODS). The index is in the main index table space. The killer here is index - at a high volume retail site you can easily notice that the data table space increases gradually as the PSA grows, but the index increase rapidly. Therefore, it should not be assumed that if the data table space is small, PSA data is only taking up a small proportion of your disk space.

Question 47: How to send Master Data Manually via IDoc

How can you send master data manually via IDoc?

A: For sending material master data follow the steps:

1. Choose: General -> Material -> Send.
2. Enter the following data:
   a. The material that you have created.
   b. Message type: MATMAS for R/3 standard, ARTMAS for R/3 Retail
   c. A target system.
   d. If you want to send configuration values for material variants in the IDoc of the material master record, activate the Send Material Completely indicator. Specify the application server you want to use.
   e. If you want to send more than one material at a time. Specify the number of materials that you want to send together.
3. Choose Execute

You can find the General -> Material -> Send at: SAP Menu -> Tools -> ALE -> Master Data Distribution -> Cross-Application -> Material -> Send or you can simply run BD10 t-code.

Question 48: How to Create New Price List Type

How can you create a new price list type?

A: Depending on your company's pricing policies, you can define your own price list types to suit the needs of your business. For example, you can define price list types by customer groups (wholesale, retail, and so on) and by currency (price lists for each foreign country you deal with). Condition records are created for each price list type. You do this using the same organizational data as for material prices (sales organization, distribution channel). You can then assign price list types to each customer in their master record.

- Condition table 006 (price list type/currency/material)
- Condition table 306 (price list type/currency/material with release status)

You want to grant prices from a wholesale price list to customer within a given period of time, without changing the master data.

To do this, the system needs to:

- Determine the item price list type, dependent upon the customer.
- Determine the price using the price list type.

The following conditions must exist in the pricing procedure:

- PBP, PBBS

Question 49: Barcode System for SAP

How can you use barcode scanner with SAP so that you can use it to issue and receipt material instead of manual key in? In addition, how can you connect barcode to SAP? Does it need middleware to link between SAP and barcode?

A: You have 3 ways for using barcode with SAP.

The first two are with radio frequency.

1. You use sap console, which connects directly through SAP (you still need a telnet server).
2. Or you can use a middleware to connect to SAP via RFC or IDoc.

The third possible way could be that you connect any barcode device with your computer to scan anything.

Question 50: RTP Stock

What does the RTP stock mean and what is its significance?

A: RTP stock signifies returnable packaging material (e.g. special containers, cylinders etc) that needs to be returned to the vendor.

Question 51: Retail-Difference between Mer.Cat. Ref. Article and Ref. Article

Which should be created first Mer.Cat.Ref. Article or Ref. Article? As both have the same views. Why is it so that even while creating Ref.Article, one has to put merchandise category in the field on the Initial Screen?

A: To create an article first of all you need a merchandise category. Now for that MC, IS-Retail offers the possibility (not mandatory) to assign a reference article to the merchandise category. If you create the reference article from the transaction WG21/WG22 it will get a special article category although it is possible to use any article.

By doing this it will be the default reference article for that MC. If you create an article and do not want to use that ref. article, you can enter a different one in MM41 (note that empty field is the MC ref. article!).

The article you then enter can belong to different Merchandise Category.

Using the reference article can speed up creating articles and thus the usage is advisable.

Question 52: Display Components

How can you see the components of a display besides the transaction MGW3 and the mm43?

A: You can check in CS03 for the details.

Question 53: Switch IDES to Retail

Can you switch IDES system into Retail?

A: No, IDES for Retail comes separately therefore you do not have to switch.

Question 54: Material Group Hierarchy

How can you use material group hierarchy classification in access sequence of condition types (e.g. discounts) if this hierarchy is made using IS-Retail classes (026) and it is not at the price communication structure!

A: Communication structures relevant for pricing are: KOMK, KOMP, and KOMG.

Integrate the field in the appropriate communication structure by means of an INCLUDE.

For pricing, for example, you include header fields in KOMKAZ, item fields in KOMPAZ: For the field name enter the field description new fields and make sure that they begin with ZZ or YY.

The description of the individual functions will inform you about the structures into which the fields must be integrated.

Activate the structure.

Include a new field in table T681 (Table T681 defines the allowed fields for the condition tables for each application and as well as in which application a field is to be used. Depending on the allocation of fields to the individual applications, only a selected number of fields are available for the creation of a condition table. A field can be assigned to more than one application) and allocate it to the application in which is to be used.

Example-

A new field for pricing has the allocation A, V, 001.

Supplying fields within the communication structure and using them in Condition Tables.

The fields included have to be supplied in such a way that they are filled with the required document fields when the document is processed. Each routine of the individual application contains user exits defined for that specific purpose. The description of the individual functions informs you about the members contained in each user exist.

To supply the fields, proceed as follows:

Check in which source table the document field is found.

In the order header the fields are found in the following tables:

VBUK SD document: Header status and administrative data
VBAK Sales document: Header data
VBKD Sales document: Business data
KUWEV Ship-to party view of customer master
KURGV Payer view of customer master
KUREV Bill-to party view of customer master
KUAGV Sold-to party view of customer master
TVAK Sales documents: Types
TVTA Organizational unit: Sales areas

In the order item the fields are found in the following tables:

VBAP Sales document: Item data
VBAPD Dynamic part: Order items
TVAP Sales documents: Item types

In the billing document header the fields are found in the following tables:

VBRK Billing document: Header data
KUWEV Ship-to party view of customer master
KURGV payer view of customer master

KUREV Bill-to party view of customer master
KUAGV Sold-to party view of customer master
VBKD Sales document: Business data
VBAK Sales document: Header data (for creation, not for change)

In the billing document item the fields are found in the following tables:

VBRP Billing document: Item data
VBAP Sales document: Item data (only for creation)

For partners the fields are found in the internal table XVBPA of the structure VBPAVB.

Supply the new field by means of a MOVE command in the defined user exit.

The routines for the supply of the new fields in order processing are found in member MV45AFZZ. The MOVE command for the supply of the new field ZZAUGRU would be:

FORM USEREXIT_PRICING_PREPARE_TKOMK.
MOVE VBAK-AUGRU TO TKOMK-ZZAUGRU.
ENDFORM.

In table T681F allocate the new field to the usage and the application area, in which it is to be used.

Question 55: Material Group Hierarchy Level

What is the Material Group hierarchy level? How can you activate it?

A: Material Group hierarchy is an IS-Retail functionality. Transaction WWG1 can be used to access it.

Question 56: New Fields in New Sub Screen of Material Master

How can you add new customized fields in the purchasing screen of material master?

A:

1. Create your own Function Group. For this, go to SPRO --> Logistics General --> Material Master --> Configuring the Material Master --> Create Program for Customized Sub screens.
2. Go to SE80 and type in your Function Group Name. Select it and do a right-click. Select More Functions --> Rebuild Object List. This will show all the objects in your Function Group. Activate your Function Group.
3. In SE80, go to Sap's Function Group MGD1 (for Industry) or MGD2 (for Retail) and copy one of the Purchasing Screens (that looks a bit similar to your new custom screen that you are going to build) to your Function Group.
4. In your Function Group, make appropriate custom changes to the screen. Add code logic if needed.
5. Go to SPRO --> Logistics General --> Material Master --> Configuring the Material Master --> Define Structure of Data Screens for Each Screen Sequence. Select: 21 Std ind. (short) tab pages (for industry) or any other appropriate selection depending on your business type.
6. Double-Click Data Screens on the hierarchy list and select Purchasing.
7. Double-Click Sub screens on the hierarchy list.
8. Replace Sap's entry: SAPLMGD1 0001 with your Function Group and Screen Names. You should now be able to view your fields on Material Master.

Question 57: Sales Tax on MRP

Is it so that MRP refers to Material Requirements Planning, which is purely the tool to manage the material requirements planning?

A: No, MRP is nothing related to material requirement planning it just stands for Maximum Retail Price and in Purchase the CST (JIP1) is calculated on MRP price not on Basic Price.

Question 58: MWST Error

Under what situations should the following pricing condition exist?

If tax EXEMPT is selected for 'imported from' and 'sold country', will it still ask MWST pricing condition while calculating pricing?

A: There are a few steps to check your VAT-settings:

1. Plant is defined at the item level. If you don't define the plant, your system will never know from where is it delivering?
2. Check your customer master, transaction XD02. At the billing tab you have to define tax classification to your customer.
3. Check the material master, transaction MM02 (retail MM42). At the sales tab you have to define tax classification to your material.
4. Check pricing master data, transaction VK12, select MWST.

Depending on your need, domestic sales or export sales, check key combinations.

Example domestic:

Country
Customer tax code
Material tax code
Tax code

Question 59: Organization Structure

What can be the right structure for a retail operating in multiple countries and with multiple autonomous business outlets? If Enterprise prefers to have separate management accounts, P&L and Balance sheet at each unit level what should be company code? What should be business area? Is it easy to generate P&L and B&Shee? Can you generate full-fledged Balance sheet at Profit center level?

A: The function of business areas is to create balance sheets and Profit and Loss statements below the company code level. Some common uses of business areas are to produce divisional financial statements or SEC segment-level reporting. It is important to note that business area functionality can be duplicated using Profit Center Accounting. The decision to use or not to use business areas should be made early on in the design phase of your project. Many new projects are leaning away from business areas and toward profit centers, but ultimately, the decision is an individual project decision based on what fits in to the overall system design of the project implementation. Some of the deciding factors are the need to report on business lines across company codes, the need for full balance sheets at the divisional or business line level, as well as the cost and benefits of business areas versus profit centers.

Question 60: Valuation at Company Code Level - Effect in P

What problem could occur if 'valuation level' is set at 'company code level' in a manufacturing company? Why does SAP Help suggest that when costing is to be applied, production valuation should be at 'plant level'?

A: For manufacturing the valuation is at `plant level' not at 'company level' as manufacturing cost (processing cost) differs from plant to plant and depends upon its resources, hence it will differ if all these plants belongs to the same company code. To avoid this valuation is at 'plant level' for PP.

Question 61: COPA in Retail System

Is it feasible to use profitability analysis in retail system in SAP retail environment?

A: Yes it is possible to use it for merchandise category reporting when you just have sales in the category and you have costs booked to a particular account. You do however have to worry about performance so it cannot be very feasible.

Question 62: SAP WAS 6.x with Enterprise 47X200 SR1

If notes state that:

Enterprise 47x200 SR1 is based on WAS 6.40 and others say it is based on WAS 6.30, how can you make out what the system is using?

A: After certain patch level Basis, WAS 620 becomes WAS 630 (though not shown in the system).

Here is the thing:

SAP Kernel WAS 640
SAP_BASIS 620 0049 SAPKB62049 SAP Basis Component
SAP_ABA 620 0049 SAPKA62049 Cross-Application Component
SAP_APPL 470 0022 SAPKH47022 Logistics and Accounting
SAP_HR 470 0035 SAPKE47035 Human Resources
ABA_PLUS 100 0011 SAPKGPBA11 PLUGIN ZU ABA_PLUS
EA-IPPE 200 0014 SAPKGPIB14 EA-IPPE 200: Add-On Installation
PI 2004_1_470 0002 SAPKIPZI52 R/3 Plug-In (PI) 2004.1 for R/3 Enterpri
PI_BASIS 2004_1_620 0005 SAPKIPYI55 Basis Plug-In (PI_BASIS) 2004_1_620
EA-APPL 200 0008 SAPKGPAB08 SAP R/3 Enterprise PLM, SCM, Financials
EA-DFPS 200 0008 SAPKGPDB08 SAP R/3 ENTERPRISE DFPS
EA-FINSERV 200 0008 SAPKGPFB08 SAP R/3 Enterprise Financial Services
EA-GLTRADE 200 0008 SAPKGPGB08 SAP R/3 Enterprise Global Trade
EA-HR 200 0016 SAPKGPHB16 SAP R/3 Enterprise HR Extension
EA-PS 200 0008 SAPKGPPB08 SAP R/3 Enterprise Public Services
EA-RETAIL 200 0008 SAPKGPRB08 SAP R/3 Enterprise Retail

Question 63: Implementation

A company had to implement SAP-BW for one of the retail industry in Korea. Since the retail company had there own BW system in china, which they also wanted to implement in Korea. It was done by copying the SAPBW templates from China to Korea (they had to implement the same cubes in Korea too). However, the problem arises when source system gets changed in Korea.

How can you activate and install those same cubes, and how can you activate and install business cubes with data? The cubes are ort_c01 and Fiap_c03 and other retail industry cubes.

A: The situation could be handled in following way:

Create an info area for Korea, using the template provided from China implementation, and then create Z info cubes in Korea info area.

Assuming here that, Korea implementation is a different from China implementation.

Question 64: Direct Deliveries to Stores in IS-Retail

If you are working for Retail and in the normal process all your goods go through your warehouse, but you have to deal with direct deliveries from your suppliers to the store as well.

You have built the following process:

- The supplier delivers directly to the store.
- The next day the supplier sends a file to head office with a consolidated invoice for all stores. In the file there is as well a part with the delivered quantities to the stores.
- The file is checked technically and then uploaded to create a Purchase Order for an administrative DC.

- The admin department checks the PO and after confirmation the file is uploaded once more --> the goods receipt is posted, the invoice verification is done and the stock transport orders to the individual stores are created as well.

The problems with this process are:

- The set up cost for the supplier are high.
- There are too many files for the admin department.
- The Appl. Man Support is a major cost as well.
- The stock in the stores is not accurate for these articles.
- The application to upload and split the file to be able to upload goods receipt and invoice receipt is outdated.

Tell what standard SAP is using as best practice or is there a smart work around for this?

A: You can have several approaches depending on the article characteristics:

- There are articles that are directly replaced in the shelves by the vendors. In these cases a purchase order is created in the store with the delivered items and quantities. The goods receipt is posted in the store. Every day, all documents (purchase orders and material docs) are sent to the central office for invoice verification.
- In other cases the purchase orders are created centrally and sent to the vendor. When the vendor arrives to the store the goods receipt is posted. Every day all documents (purchase orders and material docs) are sent to the central office for invoice verification.

In some cases vendor invoices are consolidated, in others they are not. However, SAP manages both the cases.

Question 65: How to Handle Advance Payment at POS Inbound

How can you handle the Cash advance payment if you are using Article Aggregated Sales control for POS inbound, e.g. Customer made payment for Article A on 10th Jan. 05 but due to non-availability of stock, store was able to deliver the item on 1st Feb. 05? How will you upload this sale to SAP?

A: You can follow the following steps:

1. Create DIEN article for ADVANCE PAYMENT
2. Create another Means of Payment, called "ADVANCE PAYMENT"
3. Customer made payment on 10.Jan.05 for article ADVANCE PAYMENT, and POS should capture information for which product, and details are sent back to SAP. Advance Payment receipt will be used to redeem the goods.

At SAP, once the trx is loaded, there will be an accounting journal like this:

Dr. Normal MOP (Cash, Visa, MC, etc.)
Cr. ADVANCE PAYMENT
On 1.02.2005, customer will use the advance payment receipt to redeem the goods, it is recognized as MOP = Advance Payment at POS

Once trx loaded to SAP, there will be accounting journal:

Dr. ADVANCE PAYMENT
Cr. SALES
Cr. TAX

Question 66: IS-R HPR

What is the functionality of HPR (High Performance Retail)?

A: HPR in Retail consists of programs specifically on the SAP to POS/BOS interface to improve the runtime of Master data (e.g. Article master/assortment list) IDoc generation. These programs are more efficient than the standard SAP programs. However, the end results are not exactly identical.

Question 67: Delivery Address for Customer in PO

Why the Delivery Address tab in tx ME21N (4.7 IS-Retail) does not have the customer field available as it was with previous releases, even if the settings of customer field in PO field selections is changed from 'optional' to 'required'?

A: While working with a third party, the customer field in the delivery address is not much required, yet you can set the accounting category as 'S' and then the starting point will be a sales order.

Question 68: Defining a Store

How do you set up a store in R/3 to be used in the retail system?

A: You can use TCode WB01 to create a store (In SAP retail store is a master data).

Question 69: Difference between SD/MM and IS-Retail

What are the major differences between SD/MM and IS-Retail?

A: Some differences between SD/MM and IS-Retail are as follows:

- IS-Retail was originally developed to meet specific needs of Retail industry where standard SD/MM cannot.

Significant functionality differences are:

- Store specific features are in built in IS-Retail where as it is not so in Standard SD/MM.
- Mass processing of pricing is a feature of IS-Retail (later some of the retail features were included as standard SAP (4.6))
- Assortment handling is not present in standard SAP

There are some other differences in inventory costing/valuation etc.

Question 70: Hardware Sizing

Are there any specific concerns should be taken into account regarding SAP IS-Retail hardware sizing?

A: Retail, as high volume business, has a number of specific processes. In general, you can map a high number of them to the Quick Sizer, but for some specific sizing guidelines apply.

There is a dedicated retail offline questionnaire available at service.sap.com/sizing -> sizing guidelines -> solutions % platform but ID is required.

Question 71: How to Limit the Number of Items (lines) in PO

If an external WMS system can take PO items only up to 300. Is there any way in the config or any user exit to limit the items to 300?

How can you limit the number of items in a PO created during MRP/replenishment?

A: Yes, you can limit the number of items in a user exit through following ways:

- Exit_Sapmm06e_017: user exit on item level: program a warning when allowed number of items exceeded.
- Exit_Sapmm06e_012: user exit on header level at moment of save: program an error when allowed number of items exceeded.
- And to limit the number of items in a PO created during MRP/replenishment, you should look for a user exit or you may enhance standard SAP.

Question 72: WM and Retail IS

In 4.6 and above, is there a WM/Retail industry solution distinct from the standard WM solution?

A: No, there is no difference in WM for IS-Retail in the application or in customizing.

Question 73: IS-Retail-Retail IDES or Pre-configured System

Is there a pre-configured SAP IS-Retail system available? Can you start implementation with this pre-configured system and is it possible to copy the Dev system with the data into the Prd using client copy?

A: Yes, a pre-configured SAP IS-Retail system is available, it is provided as a sample best practices setup. For more information you can contact your local SAP.

Yes, you can start implementation with this pre-configured system and technically it is possible to copy the Dev system with the data into the Prd using client copy, etc.

Question 74: Display Sets Issue

If the display sets are not exploding into the component parts at goods receipt by store and thus they go to zero stock at store because of the missing Table V_TWZLA in the plant and sales org, how can you populate/maintain Table V_TWZLA?

A: Follow this route to customize:

In customizing go to:

Logistics - General ---> Material Master ---> Retail-Specific Settings ---> Settings for structured materials ---> Structured material in logistics process.

Here you can specify if the structured material is going to explode in the purchase order or at GR. You can control this at plant category level (Store or DC).

Question 75: More IS-Retail Questions

What is the difference between MIRO, MIRA, and MRHR?

A: MRHR is the old style of doing invoice processing in SAP, which was before versions 4.0B. Then onwards SAP programmers have innovated in lots of shortcomings of the transaction. Hence they came up with MIRO, this is called Logistic Invoice Verification now. This will remain in new versions. Functionality is the same in MRHR and MIRO except the variant selection, whereas MIRA is verification in background.

Question 76: Loyalty Card in IS-Retail

How to manage loyalty card for consumer customer in SAP Retail?

Scenario:

The consumer buys article in the store and if he has the card, he will have a score and/or a price reduction. Which is the better option for managing this kind of card, as credit card with the type KK or to create a permanent article coupon?

A: SAP is coming out with a separate engine for loyalty management. As of now it is out of SAP.

Question 77: 0 Records while Extraction for 2LIS_02_ITM and 2LIS_02_HDR

What should be done if you are not getting any data thru extractor checker for the data sources 2LIS_02_ITM, and 2LIS_02_HDR, and for some other customer specific data source related to purchase orders?

A: Follow these steps:

1. Find out if your extractor is active or not (green light on)
2. Next initialize your 2Lis_* table.
3. Then fill the set up table.
4. Start with transaction LMBW and go on.
5. Once the job is run to fill the tables, go to RSA3 and check whether data is available.
6. Go to BW side and replicate.

Follow the steps and you will get the data.

Question 78: Edit Material Master Data using LSMW

You have SAP R/3 4.6b for retail and LSMW 1.8.0. How can you update material master data using LSMW? If while updating the fields SEASON CATEGORY (MARA-SAISO) and SEASON YEAR (MARA-SAISJ) during batch input processing you encounter an error such as "No batch input data for screen SAPLMGMW 4008".

A: You can use transaction MM17 (Material mass update) to update material master data. There is a limit on the number of records that can be updated.

Question 79: User Exit after PO Save

Is there any user exit after the purchase order is saved, so that you can approve a PO in synchronous mode?

A: Check the following user exit:

MMFAB001 User exit for generation of release order
LMEDR001 Enhancements to print program
MM06E005 Customer fields in purchasing document
AMPL0001 User sub screen for additional data on AMPL
LMEDR001 Enhancements to print program
LMELA002 Adopt batch no. From shipping notification when posting a GR
LMELA010 Inbound shipping notification: Transfer item data from IDoc
LMEQR001 User exit for source determination
LMEXF001 Conditions in Purchasing Documents without Invoice Receipt
LWSUS001 Customer-Specific Source Determination in Retail
M06B0001 Role determination for purchase requisition release
M06B0002 Changes to comm. structure for purchase requisition release
M06B0003 Number range and document number
M06B0004 Number range and document number
M06B0005 Changes to comm. structure for overall release of requisn.
M06E0004 Changes to communication structure for release purch.doc.
M06E0005 Role determination for release of purchasing documents
ME590001 Grouping of requisitions for PO split in ME59
MEETA001 Define schedule line type (backlog, immed. req., preview)
MEFLD004 Determine earliest delivery date f. check w. GR (only PO)
MELAB001 Gen. forecast delivery schedules: Transfer schedule implem.
MEQUERY1 Enhancement to Document Overview ME21N/ME51N
MEVME001 WE default quantity calc. and over/ under delivery tolerance

MM06E001 User exits for EDI inbound and outbound
purchasing documents
MM06E003 Number range and document number
MM06E004 Control import data screens in purchase order
MM06E005 Customer fields in purchasing document
MM06E007 Change document for requisitions upon conversion
into PO
MM06E008 Monitoring of contr. target value in case of release
orders
MM06E009 Relevant texts for "Texts exist" indicator
MM06E010 Field selection for vendor address
MMAL0001 ALE source list distribution: Outbound processing
MMAL0002 ALE source list distribution: Inbound processing
MMAL0003 ALE purchasing info record distribution: Outbound
processing
MMAL0004 ALE purchasing info record distribution: Inbound
processing
MMDA0001 Default delivery addresses
MMFAB001 User exit for generation of release order
MRFLB001 Control Items for Contract Release Order

Question 80: Help with Price List Functionality

What is the function of Price list? How can the price list type
assigned to the customer master be used in pricing and how can
you maintain a price list for a particular material?

A: Depending on your company's pricing policies, you can
define your own price list types to suit the needs of your
business. For example, you can define price list types by
customer groups (wholesale, retail, and so on) and by currency
(price lists for each foreign country you deal with). Condition
records are created for each price list type. This can be done
using the same organizational data as for material prices (sales
organization, distribution channel). You can then assign price list
types to each customer in their master record.

Question 81: Is Crystal Report a good Solution for SAP BW 3.1

What kind of tool is a Crystal Report, if it is to be used for BW front-end for developing some complex formatted reports?

With SAP configuration:
BW 3.1
SAP Retail IS (4.7)

A: For formatted and static reports Crystal is a good tool.

Advantages of Crystal Report:
Fully BW integrated
Lots of functions for creating reports and distributing reports

However, it is mainly for formatted and static reporting

Question 82: Loans Management

Is the Loans Management component of SAP (CML) something that can be used by retail organizations that have pretty extensive loan activities, or is it suitable just for banks? Where can you find book or white paper on CML?

A: TR-LM is a functionality that is capable of handling internal loans (to employees), external loans given or obtained. It is also capable of linking internal and external loans (company-sponsored loans to employees). This is suitable for banks as well as retail organizations with extensive loan activities and if you have SAP All-In-One license you should be able to implement and utilize it without additional fees (except consulting to implement).

SAP Knowledge Warehouse is the best place to find book or white paper on CML.

Question 83: Generic Material Type

What is the use of Generic Material type? Explain with example.

A: Use of retail Generic Material type can be explained the following example:

If we consider Jell-O's 70g package as the generic and all its flavors of same size as variants of the generic. Then while purchasing, they purchase the generic, which will allow mixed quantities of the variants on the order line.
They may need to buy 100 cases at a time but they only need to buy a fraction of that qty in a particular flavor (variant).

Question 84: Setting Retail Switch

What is the transaction of setting R/3 system as a retail system?

A: SPRO after import is the transaction of setting R/3 system as a retail system.

Question 85: Export as a Distribution Channel

If a customer has 3 divisions in the former system: D1, D2 and D3, where D3 is export for the old system and has D1 and D2 divisions as subordinate level and the client would like to reflect export as an organizational unit.

Which would be the better option to reflect export?

1. As a distribution channel or
2. Through the different document types created for export?

A: You can have 2 sales organizations:

1. Domestic &
2. Exports

Then have distribution channels as:

1. Distribution agents
2. Retail
3. Direct sales/Institutional sales (big companies en -gross)

You can use these divisions for different product types.

Question 86: What are EDI 850 and 875?

What are EDI 850 and 875 transmissions?

A: 850 is EDi standard document for Retail Purchase Order and 875 is EDi standard document for Grocery Purchase Order.

Question 87: LSMW - Which LSMW for Retail

Which LSMW import method should you use if you need to upload about 30,000 articles to a retail system?

A: You can use Business Object Method:

- Object: BUS1001001
- Method: CLONE
- Message type: ARTMAS
- Basic type: ARTMAS04

Question 88: Sales Order

Is it possible to have delivery and billing created automatically when the cashier generates sales order?

A: In standard 4.6 there is a standard SD document type for Cash Sales. Doc type BV creates the delivery on the spot and a receipt. An actual FI posting in billing happens during batch processing.

Question 89: IS-Retail Material

How can you have 2 descriptions in 2 languages using SAP Retail 4.7? As IDoc can carry only one language at one time in terms of the languages used in store.

A: 'Description language' sent to the store is controlled by the language defined in the store master data. You can define only one language for one store. Hence, you can send only one description to one store. However, you can define different languages for different stores and send different descriptions. The other option is that you can extend the IDoc segments to send the additional description.

Question 90: What is IS-RETAIL?

What is IS-RETAIL?

A: It is an industry solution. This means it is R/3 instances with special retail configuration and customization installed right after installation.

Question 91: Using Characteristic in Formula

If you are using a characteristic in formula in a retail sales scenario and you have 'showroom area' as navigation attribute of customer and sales value as key figure. How can you calculate sales/sq meter of showroom area?

A: To calculate sales/sq meter of showroom area create a "Replacement Path" formula from the formula selection screen. Select the characteristic and the attribute. Then use it in your formula. When executing the query the variable will be filled with the value of the attribute.

Question 92: Automatic Activation of Master Data from M Version

Retail Scenario:

Frequency of generation of material codes and customer codes is pretty high. In addition, the changes to these masters are frequent. While you are able to automate data transfer thru delta mechanism, the modified data remains in M version in BW unless manually activated.

How can you automate the modified data in M version in BW?

A: Steps to automate the modified data in M version in BW:

RSA1 > Tools > Apply Hierarchy/Attribute Change Run.

Question 93: MRP Help

Scenario:

If there are 75 retail locations that are individual plants and you are trying to run MRP on all materials that are not ordered through your DC but direct from the vendor. You have the same materials in all plants but when MRP generates req's it does by plant. Therefore, you end up with 75 req's on the same material. Is there a way for MRP to propose one req for all plants?

A: No, there is no such standard feature in SAP since SAP runs at either plant location, or storage location (MRP Area).

Question 94: How to Delete or Inactivate a Storage Location

How can you delete or inactivate a storage location if transactional data still exists for that SLOC?

A:

1. Restrict the users from posting any material document by maintaining authorization check at storage location level. Use path in SPRO ---> Materials management ---> Inventory Management & Physical inventory ---> Authorization Management ---> Authorization check at storage location.

2. If you are using external procurement, go to the MRP2 View of the material master and maintain the field 'Storage loc. for EP'. This will default the storage location to the planned order or PR and then on to the PO. Upon the receipt, the material will be received to the correct storage location. You also need to move existing stock from the old location to the new location by material transfer 311, remove the bin location and mark the old storage location for deletion

3. Use Transaction Code MM06 to set a deletion flag for material at storage location level. This shall be done for all materials that have this storage location that can be found by checking the table MARD with SE16. As well the message M7 127 from warning to error message (transaction OMCQ) must be changed.

Question 95: Retail Outbound

In POS outbound flow, is it possible to create receiver ports for each store that exists?

A: You can create as many Ports as you like by using Store Group/Dept/MC. For example, if you have 4 stores among which the three of them (i.e. 1, 2, & 3) are selling the same merchandising, then you can create one port and transmit the data through it. The respective POS will take their file because the POS server doesn't take or differentiate between IDoc numbers.

Question 96: How to set MAP equal to LAST GR/Invoice Verification

Is it a good idea to use MAP to show the LAST GR/Invoice Verification value (cost), because due to increasing drop of your local currency against the US Dollar the average price will not show your true margins against sale price?

A: It is true to say that your specific requirement cannot be met since in regard to MAP, the price will be updated subject to the stock movement and payment postings. Therefore, the other alternative is to use standard cost instead of MAP.

Question 97: Screen exit for Material Master

What are the existing screen exits for the material master in SAP version 4.5B?

A: You can check the following:

FM EXIT_SAPLOMCV_001. It is used in screen building of MM transactions.

Also check all the functions starting with EXIT_SAPLM*.

Index